Remarks by the Honorable Justice W. Michael Gillette

AUGUST 3, 1990
AT THE DEDICATION CEREMONY
OF THE JAPANESE AMERICAN HISTORICAL PLAZA
TOM McCALL WATERFRONT PARK
PORTLAND, OREGON

Secretary Roberts, Consul General Watanabe, Commissioner Lindberg, Distinguished Guests, Ladies and Gentlemen:

It is not entirely clear to me why a person of my age and experience would be asked by Mr. Naito to be the representative of the Oregon Supreme Court at this special dedication. Certainly there are a number of others who would be well suited to speak here, many individuals who began their legal careers prior to the Japanese internment. But perhaps in one sense it is symbolic that I am asked, because I represent a newer generation, a generation that stands in danger of forgetting the lessons of the Japanese internment.

It also strikes me as interesting that the Bill of Rights would be located at the [south] side of this Plaza, and the Congressional apology and the letter from the President of the United States apologizing for the Japanese internment would be at the [north] end of the Plaza—indicating, even today, the gap between our appreciation and understanding of the Bill of Rights on the one hand, and our actions on the other.

I take as a text today a line from the great American judge, Learned Hand, who wrote: "Liberty lies in the hearts of men and women. When it dies there, no constitution, no law, no court can save it. While it lies there it needs no constitution, no law, no court to save it." We meet today to dedicate a memorial to an awful period of American history, a period in which liberty died in the heart of the American people. It died in the heart of a President who ordered the imprisonment of over 110,000 people. It died in the heart of the Congress that concurred in and endorsed that imprisonment. And, saddest of all from my point of view, it died in the heart of the United States Supreme Court, which incredibly declared that the Constitution permitted that imprisonment.

And yet people will say that all that is in the past, and that surely, with the Congress' apology and with the President's apology, the matter is remedied. (The Supreme Court would apologize as well, I think, if it only had a case that gave it the opportunity to do so). So why do we need a memorial? What is the reason for creating a memorial?

And it seems to me that the answer to that is clear. Because without a memorial, without a physical gesture of remembrance, we can, we may, we will, forget.

Already the Japanese internment experience is hardly noted in civics textbooks and in history textbooks. It is barely a footnote in college history courses, and even worse it is not mentioned at all in most law schools. Yet this story, the story as represented by the memorial we dedicate today, must not, and cannot, be lost.

I think it is true that for most Americans the liberties we enjoy under the Bill of Rights are so familiar to us, so commonplace to us, that we take it for granted.

But we must ensure that liberty will always lie in the hearts of men and women. We need to be aware of how fragile liberty is and how easily it can be taken from all of us, citizens and others alike. And that, I think, is ultimately the function of this memorial. It is a memorial to which children should come. It is a memorial to which schoolchildren should be brought. It is a memorial to which all of us who know something about the Japanese internment should return again and again to remind ourselves of how fragile the effectiveness of the Bill of Rights can be in the face of panic and public disorder.

So I am honored today, especially honored today, to share in the dedication of the Japanese American Historical Plaza. Thank you very much for inviting me to be here.

Touching the Stones

Touching the Stones
Tracing One Hundred Years of Japanese American History

Editors
Mark Sherman
George Katagiri

Poets
Lawson Inada
Shizue Iwatsuki
Masaki Kinoshita
K.O. Lee
Hisako Saito

Project Consultants
Robert and Judy Murase
Bill Naito
Homer and Miyuki Yasui

Book Design
Joseph Erceg

Photographers
Stephen Cridland
Joseph Erceg
C. Bruce Forster
Timothy Hursley
Greg Kozawa
Robert K. Murase

Sources of Historical Photographs
National Japanese American Historical Society
Oregon Historical Society
Seiichi Konno
University of Washington Libraries
Yasui Collection

An Oregon Nikkei Endowment Book
Copyright ©1994
International Standard
Book Number 0-9644806-1-1
Library of Congress Catalog
Card Number 94-73984
Planned and produced by
Oregon Nikkei Endowment
P.O. Box 3458
Portland, Oregon 97208

All rights reserved. No part of this publication may be reproduced, stored in a retrieval system or transmitted in any form or by any means, electronic or mechanical, including photocopying, recording, or by any information storage and retrieval system, without the written permission from the publisher and copyright holder.

CONTENTS

7
Prologue

11
Issei Beginnings

19
Nisei Children

27
World War

35
Evacuation

43
Out to the Deserts

51
Questions of Loyalty

59
Ten Camps

65
Free Again

73
Starting Over

81
Forgetting

89
Healing

97
A Sense of the Past

103
Looking Ahead

106
Epilogue

108
About the Authors

110
Index of Sources

112
Acknowledgments

PROLOGUE

This book invites you to a place where stones are more than stones. The stones are marked with words. The words tell of lives. The lives are our own.

This book is about thirteen stones in Portland, Oregon. The words upon the stones are brief poems, poems that can be read in a moment, poems that are about passing moments in time. Yet the moments taken together trace a history of one hundred years, a history of four generations.

And this book is about the people of those generations. The *Issei:* men and women who came from Japan, who started new lives in a new country, who shared in the hopeful promise of the American West. And the *Nisei:* the American-born children of the Issei. They grew up as American citizens and came of age during the turmoil and rage of war. And the *Sansei* and *Yonsei:* the third and fourth generations, who inherited a strange legacy from American history, a legacy of loss, humiliation, exclusion and denial.

This book is about the Japanese American Historical Plaza in Portland, Oregon, where twelve granite stones rise from a low, undulating wall. The wall, composed of basalt stones, curves gently along the Willamette River esplanade. At its midpoint there is a break in the wall. Near this break stands a tall stone positioned within a circular mosaic composition of broken granite pavers. On the face of this towering, isolated stone is not a poem, but a list of ten names.

The names are of obscure places, rarely visited, places far off in America's wastelands. The names themselves are unfamiliar. Most people know nothing of their part in American history. The places no longer exist. Yet nearly every Japanese American family recalls a history of confinement in one or more of those ten obscure places. They were called "camps." Remote, desolate, harsh, often unbearable, the ten prison-cities cannot be forgotten by those who were ordered to live there. And in memories, in words, in pictures, in stone, the names are still with us.

Most of this book is like the basalt wall of the Japanese American Historical Plaza, where a one hundred year story is told in few words. The twelve poems from the granite stones mark the chapters of this book. The close standing granite stones are interconnecting narratives of Japanese American lives taken from memoirs, stories, novels, essays, and oral histories.

The center of this book, like the large standing stone, identifies the ten camps, and is devoted to recollections of camp life.

But in the end, this book is not just about Japanese Americans and the camps. It is a memorial in paper and ink form. It is a book that stands for a public need to broaden the scope of our memories, to hear new voices in our history, to see new vistas in our landscape, to touch new stones.

I

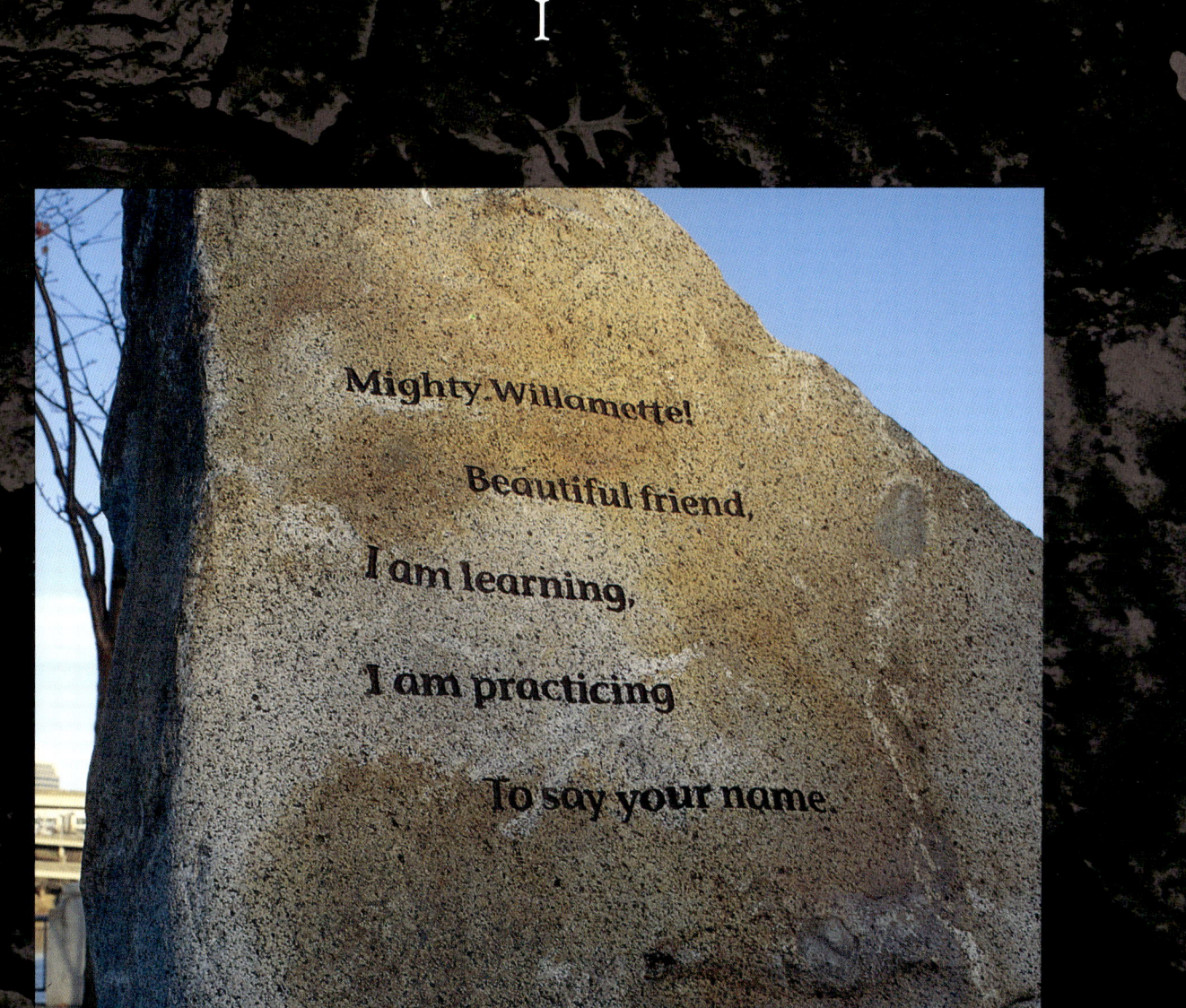

FROM JAPAN...

I still remember distinctly the feeling of the extraordinary situation of my leaving home.

I reflected on the cherished love of my parents, brothers and sisters, and the mountains and rivers where I spent such happy times, and even a flower in our garden. Trying to remember these thoughts and feelings as long as possible in my heart. It was very difficult to part from these things.

A Chinese poem came to my mind:

A young man leaves his native
  town to achieve his goal.
If he is not successful in
  his learning, even if he dies
he shall not return.

Ancestors' land is not the only place
  where you should bury your bones.
Man can be buried in any mountain
  of the world.

I suppose I did have a little bit of courage to be able to die abroad.

Yoshisada Kawai, oral history

TO AMERICA...

When the boat finally passed the Golden Gate, I had my first glimpse of San Francisco. I was on deck for hours, waiting for the golden city of dreams. I stood there with the other immigrants, chatting nervously and excitedly. First we saw only a thin shoreline. "America! America! We're in America!" someone cried. Others took up the cry, and presently the deck was full of eager faces. Finally we began to see the dirty brown hills and the houses that jutted out of the ground. This was different from what I had dreamed, and I was speechless. I had expected to see the green hills of Japan and the low sloping houses duplicated here. No, children, it wasn't disappointment exactly, but I had a lump in my throat. "This is San Francisco. My San Francisco," I murmured to myself.

What was I wearing? My best kimono, a beautiful thing. But do you know what your grandpa did when he saw me come off the boat? He looked at it and shook his head. He hauled me around as if he were ashamed of me. I could not understand.

"Never wear this thing again," he told me that night.

"Why?" I demanded. "It is a beautiful kimono."

"You look like a foreigner," he said. "You must dress like an American. You belong here."

Toshio Mori, **Tomorrow Is Long, Children**

A NEW WORLD...

My, I did all the farm work there was to do in America...Papa and I and the children going from place to place. To move was easy. All I had to do was roll up the blankets and say, "Let's go," and soon after, we were gone. Issei—it was the same for all of them. They would bring their children everywhere. "*Sa-a!*" and they would wrap their children in blankets and go.

Pear picking started in Walnut Grove. I said "Let's go." After pears came peach packing in Marysville. In Marysville the air was so stiffling hot that we would arise at three in the morning and quickly pick peaches before the sun's rays reached their peak. We lived in a vacated school house and fetched water from a well. Since there was no kitchen, we dug a hole in the earth and placed two metal bars over the hole to cook our food.

Then we worked for Masuoka-san picking peas. He planted them on the mountain's slope because they grew faster, away from the ocean fog, yet warmed from the gentle salt air. The view from the mountains was breathtaking. We would leave Nesan in the car and let her sleep while we picked peas on slopes so steep that you slipped with each step. Already my stomach bulged big with child. I worked up to the day Hana was born.

I remember when Hana arrived. The labor pains began late in the night. Papa drove me to the hospital in San Jose in a dilapidated Ford which barely made it over the hills. Each bump in the road sent a shock of excruciating pain. After I gave birth I stayed in the hospital for one week and came home to rest for another two.

I kept thinking, "I must work and go back to Japan." I was lonely—not a single relative. It might have been different had I been with someone I liked, but Papa never treated me gently. We never had conversation. We just worked and had babies.

Akemi Kikumura, her mother's story, **Through Harsh Winters**

A NEW LIFE...

"Where we lived, an odd thing used to happen," says my father, his brow wrinkling in the effort to recapture the image. "Twice a year, a Yakima Indian and his grandson would appear. They would come walking across the desert landscape: two blurred figures growing into an old man and a boy. They would come bearing a gift—an alderwood smoked salmon.

"To me, it always seemed a miracle, like the kings arriving in Bethlehem or a mirage from some desert delirium. *'Kiku, Kiku, Kikumatsu!'* they called in Japanese. 'Chrysanthemum, Chrysanthemum, Chrysanthemum-pine.' From their throats came my father's name: low and singing, like the voices of birds, like the saying of a prayer."

"Where did they come from? Why did they come?"

"They walked from the Columbia River. Each summer the Indians gathered driftwood, timbers washed ashore from overloaded logging barges. But winters were harsh and driftwood limited. Your grandfather gathered railroad ties to keep their babies warm."

"And the fish?"

"The salmons were thanksgiving. When the flickering figures appeared calling, 'Kiku, Kiku, Kikumatsu,' we all would rush outside. Your grandfather was very happy to hear the Kiku call. It was like the first sip of water in the morning of the new year: a sign of Buddha's goodness. It meant the Indians had survived."

Lydia Minatoya, **Talking to High Monk in the Snow**

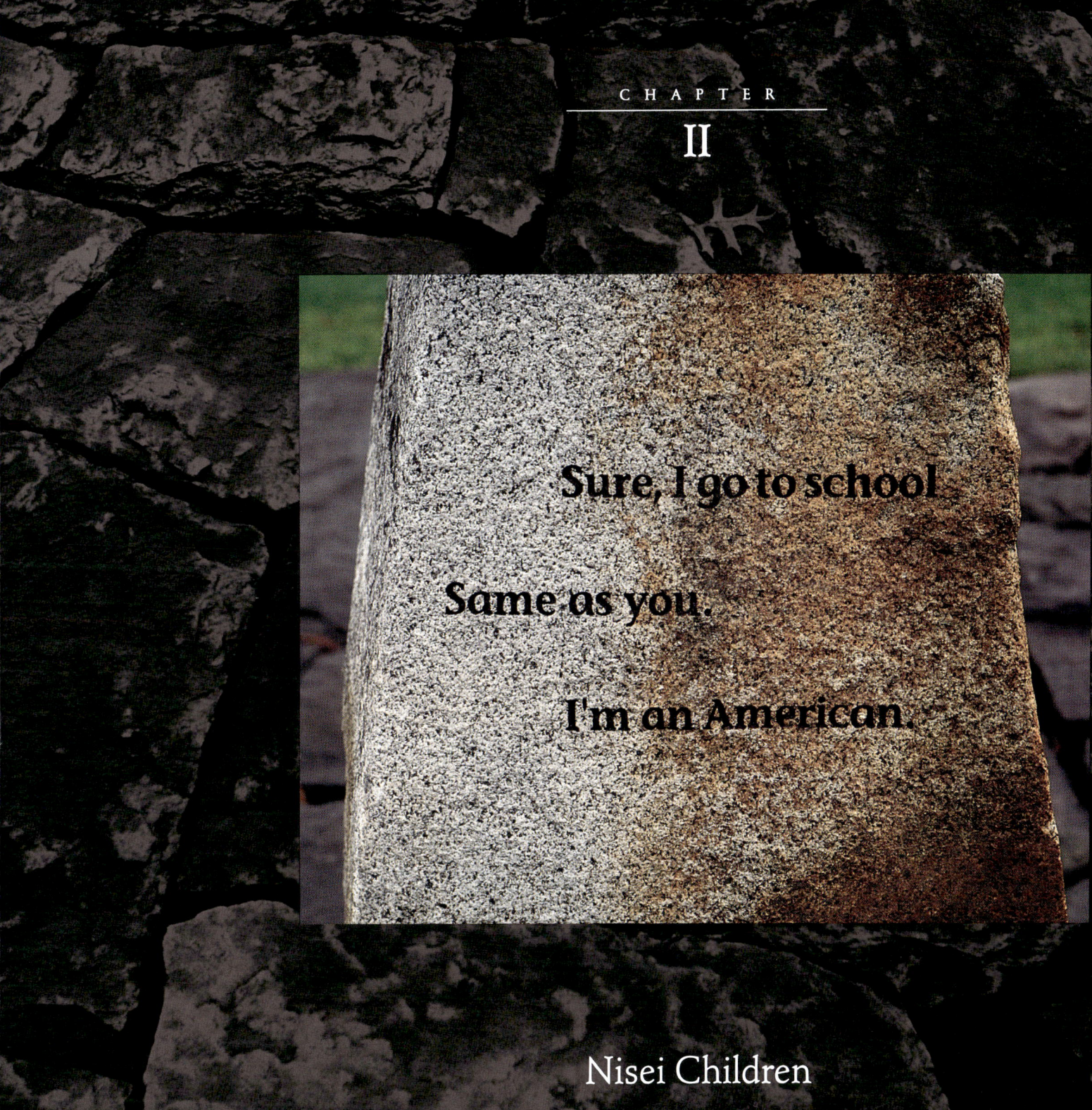

CHAPTER
II

Sure, I go to school

Same as you.

I'm an American.

Nisei Children

DOUBLE IDENTITIES...

...There was a time that I no longer remember when you used to smile a mother's smile and tell me stories about gallant and fierce warriors who protected their lords with blades of shining steel and about the old woman who found a peach in the stream and took it home and, when her husband split it in half, a husky little boy tumbled out to fill their hearts with boundless joy.

I was that boy in the peach and you were the old woman and we were Japanese with Japanese feelings and Japanese pride and Japanese thoughts because it was all right then to be Japanese and feel and think all the things that Japanese do even if we lived in America.

Then there came a time when I was only half Japanese because one is not born in America and raised in America and taught in America and one does not speak and swear and drink and smoke and play and fight and see and hear in America among Americans in American streets and houses without becoming American and loving it....

John Okada, **No-No Boy**

One day when I was a happy six-year old, I made the shocking discovery that I had Japanese blood. I was a Japanese.

Mother announced this fact to us in a quiet, deliberate manner one Sunday afternoon in the small kitchen, converted from one of our hotel rooms.

"So, Papa and I have decided that you and Ka-chan will attend Japanese school after grammer school every day." She beamed at us.

I choked on my rice.

Terrible, terrible, terrible! So that's what it meant to be Japanese—to lose my afternoon play hours! I fiercely resented this sudden intrusion of blood into my affairs.

"But, Mama!" I shrieked. "I go to Bailey Gatzert School already. I don't want to go to another!"

Father and Mother painted glowing pictures for me. Just think you'll grow up to be a well-educated young lady, knowing two languages. One of these days you'll thank us for giving you this opportunity.

But they could not convince me. Until this shattering moment, I had thought life was sweet and reasonable. But not any more. Why did Father and Mother make such a fuss just because we had Japanese blood? Why did we have to go to Japanese school? I refused to eat and sat sobbing, letting great big tears splash down into my bowl of rice and tea.

JAPANESE FAMILIES...

We sit here trying to recall our first day of school. It was so long, long ago that the events of the day itself have been forgotten. But fragmentary memories of the first year of school come back, like bits of a forgotten nightmare.

We spoke scarcely a half dozen words of English when we first entered school. We had been reared on the outskirts of a "Little Tokyo," and so we had no playmates other than little Japanese-speaking Nisei.

And our parents, who were acutely aware of the shortcomings in their English pronunciation, had hesitated to try to teach us English for fear of corrupting our accents.

We have vague recollections of sitting blankly in class and reacting to instructions partly by intuition, partly by copying the reactions of the other pupils. Most clearly, we recall the misery of shyness.

Bill Hosokawa, **"The Frying Pan"**

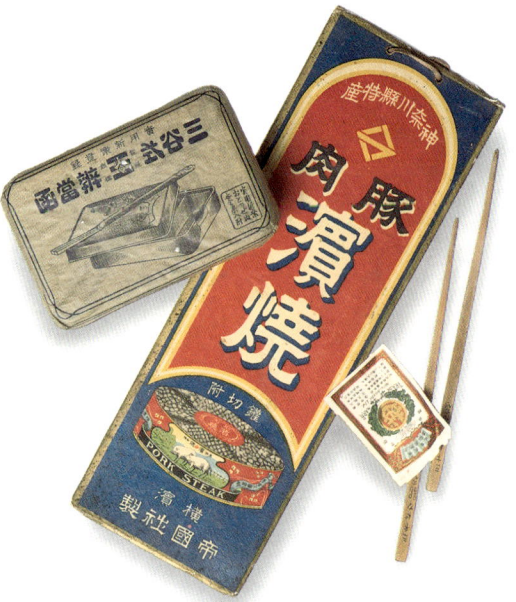

MAKING ENDS MEET...

In my junior year in high school, my dad pulled me out of school for a year because it was the worst part of the depression and the family was having a hard struggle to make both ends meet. My Dad could not afford to hire another worker so I had to step in and work. I went back to high school the next year and after that I wised up and I took a more mature attitude towards my studies and I did my homework regularly. School meant much more to me after working that year in the restaurant. It was a fad for all the Nisei to try and make the Honor Society. I tried to make it also but it was a little beyond me.

   I did not have any definite ambitions but I had secret desires to become a good writer. My greatest success in school was in the composition classes. I was taking a college preparatory course because I had vague ambitions to go to college. I did not take any extra curricular activities at all. My closest friend in school was a white kid. I just saw him around the class and we rarely had contacts after school because I still had to rush home to the restaurant.

Dorothy Swaine Thomas, interview with restaurant keeper, **The Salvage**

CHAPTER

III

World War

LIVING WITH UNCERTAINTY...

On the West Coast there was talk of possible sabotage and invasion by the enemy. It was "Jap" this and "Jap" that. Restricted areas were prescribed and many arrests took place. All enemy aliens were required to have certificates of identification. Contraband such as cameras, binoculars, short-wave radios, and firearms had to be turned over to the local police.

At this time I was working as a mosaic artist for Fort Ord and for the Serviceman's Hospitality House in Oakland, California. I was too busy to bother about the reports of possible evacuation.

However, it was not long before I realized my predicament. My fellow workers were feeling sorry for me; my Caucasian friends were suggesting that I go East; my Japanese-American friends were asking me what I would do if all American citizens and aliens of Japanese ancestry were evacuated.

Letters from a sister in Southern California informed me that Father had been whisked away.

The people looked at all of us, both citizens and aliens, with suspicion and distrust.

Mine Okubo, **Citizen 13660**

came in the morning and asked where he was. I told them I didn't know. This big bruiser of an agent, a cross between a football fullback and a Nazi stormtrooper, said "Don't get sassy with me!" He didn't call me any names, but his tone...

They surrounded the house; one agent came in from the rear, two came in from the front. The leader said, "Don't worry, we're going to take care of your father—you'll hear from us."

Just like the movies. They took him away. It was nearly a year before we were together again.

Jack Matsuoka, **oral history**

BEING A JAP...

The sneaky, little five-and-dime-store-junk-producing "Japs" had dared to attack the righteous, mighty America. The "Mongol barbarians" had launched an attack on Buck Rogers, Jack Armstrong, Bob Hope, and Shirley Temple.... How dare this nation of schoolboys, gardeners, and produce clerks attack the greatest white nation on earth! The President of the United States pronounced the attack dastardly and December 7, 1941 "a date that will live in infamy."... If there were ever a contest between good and evil, this was it.... America had democracy, God, Jesus, Hollywood, and Ralph Waldo Emerson on its side.... The "Japs" had an emperor, pagan idols, and buck-toothed, slant-eyed faces. They were a subspecies destined for servility but not yet housebroken.... The "Japs" were at best quaint, ridiculously polite, and inveterate copycats....

But being a "Jap" myself, despite my all-American convictions, I sensed contradictions in this line of reasoning. Wasn't I pretty bright? A straight-A student, only fourteen but in the tenth grade and not trying hard.... We "Japs" seemed imbued with a sense of humor. We never got messed up with the law. And in fact, our skins were not yellow, nor were our eyes slanted. Our teeth were as straight or as crooked as the next kid's.

William Minoru Hohri, **Repairing America**

LOSS OF FACE...

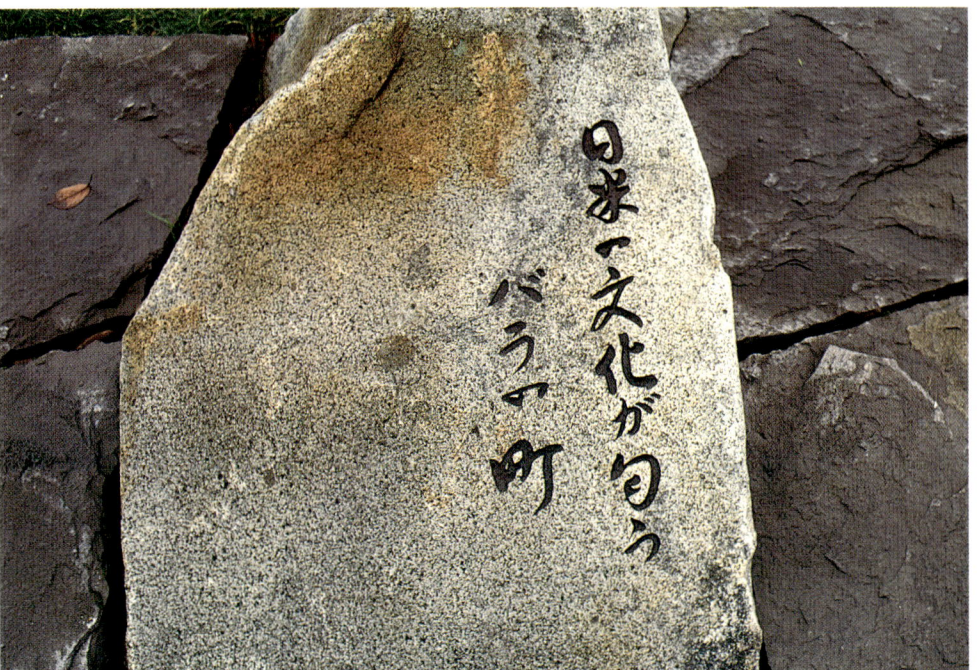

I was worried and wondered what was going on. Banks refused to let me withdraw the money I had saved. We had lived there for ten years. My six children had been able to go to any shop they wanted without money and the stores would bill me later.

But various rules were made after the outbreak of the war that prevented us from shopping....

A lot of news about the people arrested by the FBI began to be reported in the newspapers. I was afraid of getting arrested, because I had a wife and six children to support. I had already planted seedlings on fifty acres of land, and all our money was invested in the farm. What could we do if I were arrested?

So I started burying the things which might cause any trouble. Since I was practicing kendo, I had a lot of materials on it. I put those things together, dug a hole, and buried them.

Then my wife suggested that burying was not safe enough and that we should burn them. So we started burning things. Books were especially difficult to burn; so we had to tear pages piece by piece. We burned a lot of books.

But on February 21, when I came home from work, the FBI was waiting to arrest me. I will never forget that day.

Masao Hirata, **oral history**

CHAPTER

IV

Rounded up

In the sweltering yard.

Unable to endure any longer

Standing in line

Some collapse.

Evacuation

48 HOURS TO GET OUT...

The secondhand dealers had been prowling around for weeks, like wolves, offering humiliating prices for goods and furniture they knew many of us would have to sell sooner or later. [Mama tried to pack her most valuable possessions:] her pottery, her silver, kimonos Granny had brought from Japan, tea sets, lacquered tables, and one fine old set of china, blue and white porcelain, almost translucent.

On the day we were leaving, Woody's car was so crammed with boxes and luggage and kids we had just run out of room. Mama had to sell this china.

One of the dealers offered her fifteen dollars for it. She said it was a full setting for twelve and worth at least two hundred. He said fifteen was his top price.

Mama started to quiver. Her eyes blazed up at him. She had been packing all night and trying to calm down Granny, who didn't understand why we were moving and what all the rush was about. Mama's nerves were shot, and now navy jeeps were patrolling the streets. She didn't say another word. She just glared at this man, all the rage and frustration channeled at him through her eyes.

He watched her for a moment and said he was sure he couldn't pay more than seventeen fifty for that china. She reached into the red velvet case and took out a dinner plate and hurled it at the floor right in front of his feet.

The man leaped back shouting "Hey! Hey, don't do that! Those are valuable dishes!"

Mama took out another dinner plate and hurled it at the floor, then another, and another, never moving, never opening her mouth, just quivering and glaring at the retreating dealer, with tears streaming down her cheeks. He finally turned and scuttled out the door, heading for the next house. When he was gone she stood there smashing cups and bowls and platters until the whole set lay in scattered blue and white fragments across the wooden floor.

Jeanne Wakatsuki Houston, **Farewell to Manzanar**

EVACUATION
~SALE~
四十年多大の御厚情を
感謝致します
NEW STORE
8 a.m. – 6
SATURDAY
8 a.m. – 9

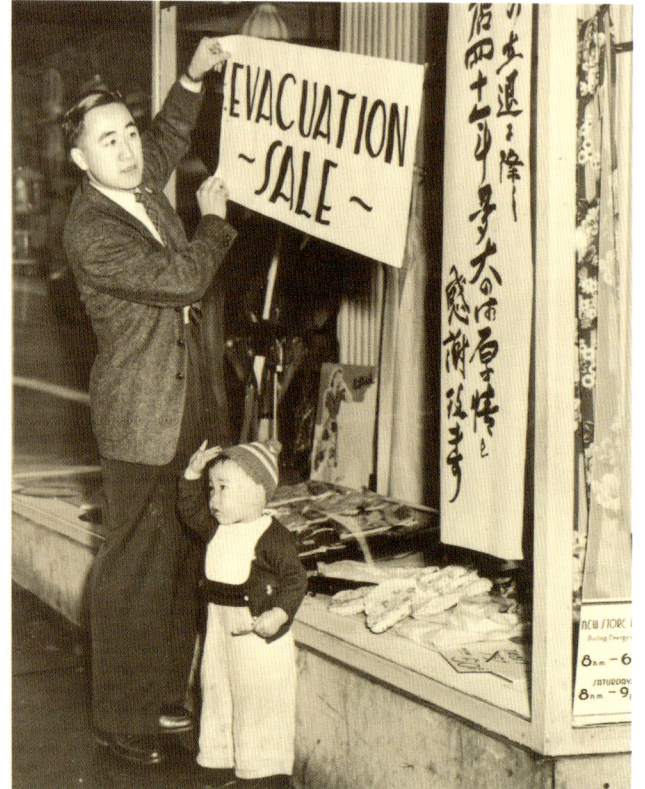

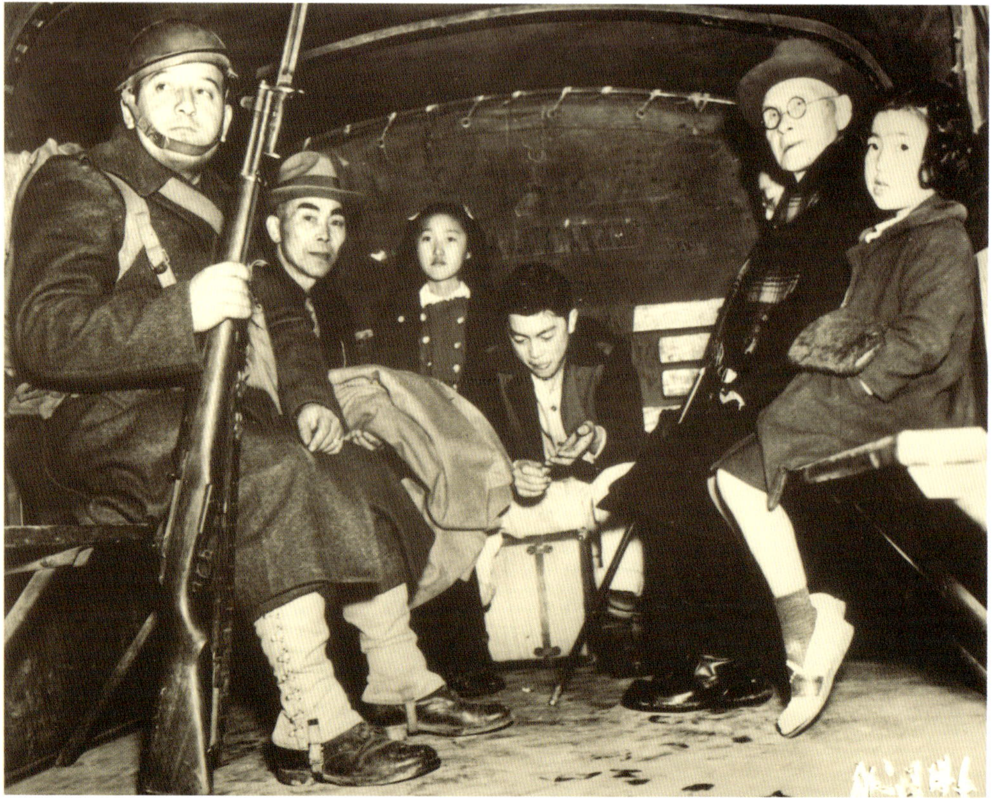

Several weeks before May, the Japanese people on the West Coast were notified to move out. Soldiers came around and posted notices on telephone poles.

It was sad for me to leave the place where I had been living for such a long time. Staring at the ceiling in bed at night, I wondered who would take care of my cherry tree and my house after we moved out. I also thought about my mother in Japan. I regretted not having returned to Japan earlier.

Soldiers came, and I was moved with the other Japanese people from Sacramento.

In my childhood in Japan a number of soldiers passed through our village once in a while. The soldiers encouraged children to become brave men. My image of Japanese soldiers was good.

However, the American soldiers who attended the evacuation were mean....

Takae Washizu, **oral history**

NEW RULES...

The sun was going down as we started along the muddy track, and a cold piercing wind swept in from the bay. When we arrived, there were six long weaving lines of people waiting to get into the mess hall. We took our place at the end of one of them, each of us clutching a plate and silverware borrowed from friends.

Shivering in the cold, we pressed close together trying to shield Mama from the wind. As we stood in what seemed like a breadline for the destitute, I felt degraded, humiliated, and overwhelmed with a longing for home.

And I saw unutterable sadness on my mother's face.

This was only the first of many lines we were to endure, and we soon discovered that waiting in line was as inevitable a part of Tanforan as the north wind that swept in from the bay stirring up all the dust and litter of the camp.

Yoshiko Uchida, **Desert Exile**

A NEW HOME...

They were taken to Tanforan Racetrack, south of the city, which was to be their new home. The stables were used as barracks, and horsestalls became "apartments" for families.

As she viewed the dirt and manure left by former occupants, she realized, "So this is what they think of me."

Realization was followed by shame. She recalled how truly she had believed she was accepted, her foolish confidence, her unfounded dreams. She and her Nisei friends had been spinning a fantasy world that was unacknowledged by the larger fabric of society. Now the damp, dusty floor and stark cots reminded her sharply of her place.

R.A. Sasaki, **"The Loom"**

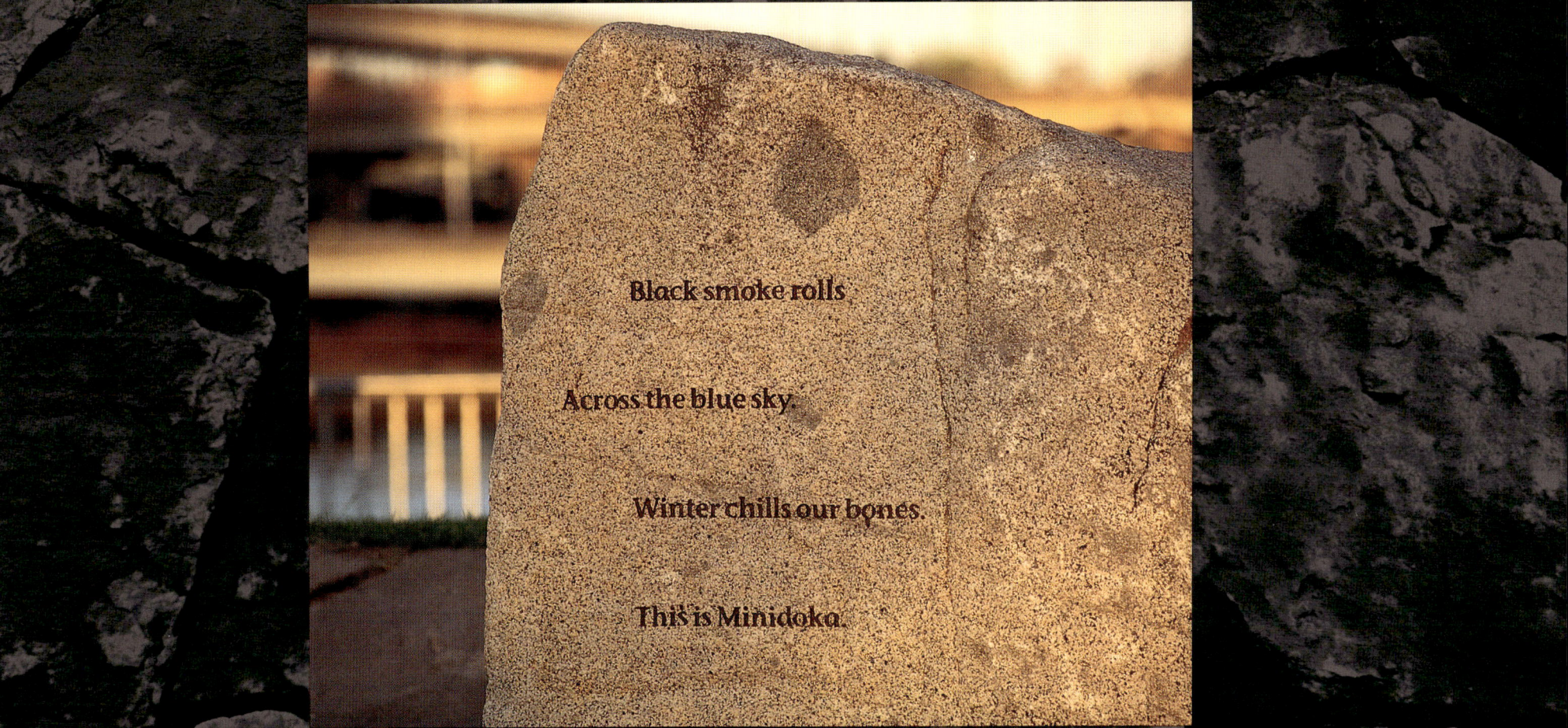

MOVING AGAIN...

We are a dismal procession. Reluctantly we step from the train onto the platform of Newell, a small town near the Oregon border; it will soon be dwarfed by our newborn city of 20,000. There are a few townspeople out to watch, wearing unfriendly expressions. We are directed to waiting buses for the final leg of our journey. It has been a long three hundred miles; a long time from yesterday to today; a long time from December to June; a long, bumpy ride along the dusty roads to Tule.

The dry heat burns the dirt loose from the earth. In gusts and whirlwinds it blows hundreds of feet above Tule, abrades our faces and filters into our eyes and throats, burning and strangling. When the spiraling wind temporarily dances away, the blue of sky descends, making bare the mountain peaks of June now spotted with barbed wire that extends across hills and valleys and sky from machine gun tower to machine gun tower.

We enter the gates: there is suddenly no past. Our lives become no more than endless corridors stretching a mile and a half into the horizon.

Edward Miyakawa, **Tule Lake**

On our first day in camp, we were given a rousing welcome by a dust storm. It caught up with us while we were still wandering about looking for our room. We felt as if we were standing in a gigantic sand-mixing machine as the sixty-mile gale lifted the loose earth up into the sky, obliterating everything. Sand filled our mouths and nostrils and stung our faces and hands like a thousand darting needles.

At last we staggered into our room, gasping and blinded. We sat on our suitcases to rest. The window panes rattled madly, and the dust poured in through the cracks like smoke. It seemed as if we had been sitting for hours in the stifling room before we were aroused by the familiar metallic clang of a dinner triangle.

The mess hall was a desolate sight with thick layers of dust covering the dining table and benches, and filling teacups and bowls. As we stood in the chow line, we stared out of the window, wondering when the storm would subside.

Just as suddenly as the storm had broken out, it died. We walked out of the mess hall under a pure blue sky, startling in its serenity.

It was as if there had been a quiet presence overhead, untouched and unaffected by the violence below, and the entire summer evening sky had lowered itself gently into a cradle of peace and

A NEW KIND OF PLACE...

If you went to an area without any trees, totally barren and full of silt knee-high, and if you went into this all by yourself—it would be a very discouraging environment, right? Well, this is the kind of environment they selected. This Poston is Indian reservation, but none of the Indians wanted it! Just barren, worse than desert, it's nothing but silt, knee-high. Just picture those barracks in that silt.

Weatherwise, I took it as it came. Dusty, stormy days where the only place you could be was in your room in the barracks, and even the barracks was no haven because all that silt was blown in.

You'd see a black cloud in the distance and that meant you take cover. And all that silt came right through the fine cracks. And when it was over, probably in about forty minutes, your bed, all your clothing was just covered with silt.

Lawrence Sasano, **oral history**

ANOTHER PART OF THE PLAN...

From the assembly centers the government herded the people into what it called "relocation centers." There were ten of these camps built to hold more than 110,000 Japanese and Japanese-Americans—many of them children. The average stay in camp was three and a half years.

No one made any effort to find out if the people they were locking up were loyal American citizens. If you had Japanese ancestry and lived on the West Coast, that was enough. You were sent to one of the camps.

The Relocation Authority told us that submitting to internment was the way we could prove our loyalty. They also said that in the detention camps, they could keep us safe from a hostile public.

There may have been some truth to that, but they were putting us in barbed-wire camps with sentry towers, the guns pointed in.

Gordon Hirabayashi, **oral history**

CHAPTER

VI

> Our young men and women
>
> Joined the army, too.
>
> They are proud to be American.

Questions of Loyalty

AMERICAN HEROES...

...I remember Kenzo, whose mother was in the hospital and did not want him to go. The doctor told him that the shock might kill her. He went anyway, the very next day, because though he loved his mother he knew that she was wrong, and she did die.

And I remember Harry, whose father had a million-dollar produce business, and the old man just boarded everything up because he said he'd rather let the trucks and buildings and warehouses rot than sell them for a quarter of what they were worth. Harry didn't have to stop and think when his number came up.

Then there was Mr. Yamaguchi, who was almost forty and had five girls. They would never have taken him, but he had to go and talk himself into a uniform.

I remember a lot of people and a lot of things now as I walk confidently through the night over a small span of concrete which is part of the sidewalks which are part of the city which is part of the state and the country and the nation that is America....

John Okada, **No-No Boy**

53

our nation.

But equally to the point, we sought to gain for our parents, our peers, ourselves, and our children the right to be treated as American equals under the law.

The Army organized Japanese Americans into the 442nd Regimental Combat Team, which fought as shock troops in eight major campaigns in Italy and France. Although the 442nd never numbered more than 3,000 men at any time, it won 18,143 individual decorations, including 9,486 Purple Hearts, and it suffered 680 dead.

Mike Masaoka, **They Call Me Moses Masaoka**

SOMETHING TO PROVE...

My Uncle Koji was an engineer, a graduate of the University of California at Berkeley. In the workplace, he found his degree had little value. In time, he found himself in camp.

Camp was tedious, and when the Wartime Relocation Authority decided to provide internees with the opportunity to declare their patriotism, Uncle Koji was eager to comply.

Loyalty was determined by responses to a long questionnaire; but the critical questions were numbers twenty-seven—"Are you willing to serve on combat duty wherever ordered?"—and twenty-eight—"Will you swear unqualified allegiance to the United States of America, defend the U.S. from all attack, forswear any allegiance to the Japanese emperor or any other foreign organization?" If you said Yes Yes, you were offered the opportunity of immediate enlistment. My uncle said No No.

"Actually, I was a No No No No Boy," he says. "That questionnaire made me so damn mad. *'If you met the emperor face-to-face would you be willing to kill him?'* The questions were ridiculous! I did not want to kill a soul.

I knew the Constitution; I'd read my Henry David Thoreau. I decided to assert myself. I decided to say No No."

Uncle Koji was declared a menace and sent off to a maximum security detention camp.

Lydia Minatoya, **Talking to High Monks in the Snow**

WE ARE YOUR CITIZENS...

It is inconceivable that any other group of Americans could have had their civil and constitutional rights so massively abused by being placed under armed guard and behind barbed wire without due process. It is inconceivable that any other group of Americans, during such an ordeal, would have volunteered for military combat and engaged in legendary acts of sacrifice and heroism to prove their worth and our worth as citizens.... They had a point to prove and they did it bravely and with honor. But frankly, it is not appropriate to make continued references to their bravery as though it were necessary for our being accepted as full citizens. We are all citizens by reason of birth and by law, not by the blood sacrificed by our brothers on the battlefield.

William Minoru Hohri, **America Repaired**

Ten Camps

GILA RIVER

It was September and the weather was mild. The sky was perfectly clear and at nightfall I looked up and saw more stars than I had ever seen in my life. They were larger and brighter than in California and one stretch of sky looked like somebody had spilled a trail of glistening talcum powder.

My brothers chose to sleep outside in the open air, but I did not join them. I was worried about wolves, coyotes, rattlesnakes, and scorpions.

At Gila there were no barbed wire fences or soldiers with guns. Instead, the desert and all its deadly creatures held us prisoner.

Gene Oishi, **In Search of Hiroshi**

GRANADA

There were good things as well as bad things. There were flowers which resembled morning glories. They were a lot bigger than morning glories and really beautiful. The roots were very big, like potatoes. They said that Indians used to make wine out of those roots. Digging the roots of the plant became very popular with the Issei.

Sadly, there were those whose minds snapped in camp, and they wandered out and died in the wilderness. There were more than several of those among the older Issei. We had to search all over for them. Sometimes those old people fell into holes and could not get out. Some of them were lucky, because we found them in time. Others died out there.

Wataru Ishisaka, **oral history**

HEART MOUNTAIN

Out of the barracks windows there was only gray sand, scudding gray clouds, gray sagebrush that stretched to the gray horizon. Gray wallboard on four walls and ceiling of our cubicle, a floor gray with the desert ground until it turned only more gray with each scrubbing.

It was Christmas and we tried to make it gay with little gifts and trinkets purchased through mail order houses, even a little artificial tree fashioned of odds and ends and draped with cotton snow.

And yet the grayness permeated the air, for we were lonely in the midst of the 10,000. It wasn't a longing for any particular friend or group of friends; it was the hollow, numbing feeling of being outcast, unwanted and forgotten. Outcast from communities where we belonged, unwanted by our nation in a war emergency, forgotten by our fellow citizens.

Bill Hosokowa, **"From the Frying Pan"**

JEROME

All of a sudden cold weather arrived, and they didn't have enough wood to heat the rooms. We were on the edge of the Mississippi River, the swamplands of Arkansas. We had to go into the woods to chop wood. All the men stopped everything. School, everything, was closed and the young people were told to go out and work.

We can stoop so low as human beings; we got so greedy and selfish. People started to hoard wood. There wouldn't be enough for some people.

When we're unhappy and miserable, our sense of values and our behavior change. We can become hateful people.

Mary Tsukamoto, **oral history**

MANZANAR

As the months at Manzanar turned to years, it became a world unto itself, with its own logic and familiar ways. In time, staying there seemed far simpler than moving once again to another, unknown place. It was as if the war were forgotten, our reason for being there forgotten. The present, the little bit of busywork you had right in front of you, became the most urgent thing. In such a narrowed world, in order to survive, you learned to contain your rage and your despair, and you try to re-create, as well as you can, your normality, some sense of things continuing.

Jeanne Wakatsuki Houston, **Farewell to Manzanar**

MINIDOKA

Winter in Minidoka was as intense an experience as summer had been. We gave a lusty cheer for the government when we were told they would provide winter clothing for those who needed it. Mother was the first to go after her clothing allotment. When she came home with the bundle, we all gathered around her excitedly to see what she had. She held up a dangling pair of long johns, olive drab army trousers of World War I, and a navy pea coat.

Sumi and I protested hysterically that we were all going to look like members of the Internal Security staff since these clothes were exactly what Father and his friends wore on patrol duty.

Henry snorted disgustedly at us, "Oh, women! Why should you care what you look like in camp?"

Even when winter swept in with wild shrieking winds and tons of snow, we remained steadfast. The dull gray-brown of the prairie disappeared, and we moved as if in a dream through a muffled white world. There was nothing but whiteness all around us, the white-mantled barracks, the white dunes, and the blank white sky.

It was only after a man living on our block became lost one night in a snowstorm and died from exposure, that we finally gave in. We ran to the clothing office, and on bended knee, begged for "Long johns, pea coat, waistcoat, anything!" The man in charge pointed to the almost empty shelves, and said laconically, "Out of luck, I'm afraid. Nothing in your size."

Monica Sone, **Nisei Daughter**

POSTON

We were worried. We didn't know what our lives would be. See, we didn't know the next day—that we worried about. We're all together in one camp; so many camps in the United States scattered all over. In Poston, 15,000 in one camp. Surrounded among the barbed wire, see. We cannot get out. And all guards standing everyplace. And we don't know what our life is going to be. I mean, are they going to kill us or…? We didn't know what the next day might be.

Frank Kadowaki, **oral history**

ROHWER

The winters were cold, but we had a big stove. A fire was always burning. People went to the mountains and collected wood. They carved and polished the wood, making *obutsudans* [Buddhist altars], drawers, chairs, all sorts of things. No matter which way you faced, there were mountains. You couldn't tell which direction was east or west. Many got lost and search parties went out to look for them. There were quite a few who died there.

Akemi Kikumura, **Through Harsh Winters**

TOPAZ

As spring made its way to our desert camp, there was only a slight touch of warmth in the air. Everywhere I looked, there was only the hard white glare of bleached sand and no sign of the renewal of life so abundant in California.

    We nurtured carefully a single daffodil bud that a friend had sent us, planting it in an old tin can and watching it closely each day. When the golden flower finally burst open, it was an occasion of real rejoicing, and I was amazed at the pleasure even a single flower could bring.

    One morning when I opened our door, I saw a flock of seagulls winging westward in the desert sky. "Come look! Hurry!" I shouted to everybody. I didn't know where they had come from or where they were going, but their shrill cries brought back with painful clarity the sounds of San Francisco Bay. For a fleeting moment I was touched by the beauty and grace of their soaring flight, and overwhelmed with thoughts of home.

Yoshiko Uchida, **Desert Exile**

TULE LAKE

"What we have to say should be listened to. It is the gap between the promise of America and its fulfillment: the fulfillment is non-existent, like the ear you give us.

    "You ask why it is we are different from the *'loyals,'* why some are fighting in Europe while others remain here. We are no different. We have had forced upon us a choice we did not wish to make. You refuse to listen to us, however many times, however many ways we tell you. You make us accept the intent of your prejudice which forces us into positions of inferiority and self-hatred, into compromise and confusion that makes bus-boys from engineers, fruit market clerks from architects, stock boys from those with college degrees, and now concentration camp inhabitants whose sons and brothers and husbands fight for this country overseas.

    "If you should look around these barracks, at babies being nursed, at the old hardly able to walk, at the masses of people, would you see them as clearly as if they were white?"

Edward Miyakawa, **Tule Lake**

THE CAMPS DISAPPEAR...

When the war ended, Poston began gradually to empty. In the block next to ours a family of Hopi Indians moved into one of the barracks. They had chickens and a pair of goats in a makeshift pen made of chicken wire. They were very friendly people and allowed us children to pat the goats.

The grandfather of the family liked to talk to us and he told us how the white man had taken their land away. One day, he said, there would be a great Indian uprising and they would take all of the land back.

Later, other Indian families began to move into the camp and sometimes late at night you could hear an Indian brave shout what might have been a war chant at the top of his lungs.

It seems eerie when I think back on our final days at Poston, on a community of imprisoned Japanese beginning to scatter, the barracks taking on a look of deterioration as the desert reasserted its claim, and the Hopi Indians, the true owners of the land, gathering slowly, prophesying war.

Gene Oishi, **In Search of Hiroshi**

The week that the government announced that we could leave the relocation camps and return to Oregon, there was much excitement in our family and certainly in all families in the camps. There were only four of our family left by this time, when Pa asked us if we wanted to go home. Pa, Dick, and I said "Yes!" but Ma said "No."

She had been reading the newspapers and her fears had been fed regularly there.

Some Japanese had already returned to their homes in California and had been greeted with vandalism, vigilantism, theft, intimidations, and so forth. In our hometown weekly paper, the Hood River News, there had been full page ads every week during January to March, 1945, warning the Japanese not to return to Hood River. "You are not wanted," they said. "If you come back, we will make life miserable for you."

Each of these ads had a short letter or statement on a theme such as "Only good Jap is a dead one," or "So sorry, Japs are not wanted in Hood River." This was followed by a petition signed by people, residents of Hood River County, many of whom we had known all our lives, as old friends or at least acquaintances.

It was bewildering and discouraging, to say the least, to peruse these columns and columns of names each week to see which of all our old friends had succumbed to the petition.

Mitzi Asai Loftus, **Made In Japan And Settled In Oregon**

LEAVING EARLY...

The day of my departure arrived. I dashed to the block manager's office to turn in the blankets and other articles loaned to me, and went to the Administration Office to secure signatures on the various forms given me the day before.

I received a train ticket and $25, plus $3 a day for meals while traveling; these were given to each person relocating on an indefinite permit.

I dashed to the mess hall for a bite to eat, then picked up my pass and ration book at the Internal Security Office, and hurried to the gate. There I shook hands with the friends who had gathered to see me off. I lined up to be checked by the WRA and the Army.

I was now *free*.

I looked at the crowd at the gate. Only the very old or very young were left.

Here I was, alone, with no family responsibilities, and yet fear had chained me to the camp. I thought, "My God! How do they expect these poor people to leave the one place they can call home."

I swallowed a lump in my throat as I waved good-bye to them.

Mine Okubo, **Citizen 13660**

CHAPTER VIII

Through the car window

A glimpse of pines.

Oregon mountains.

My heart beats faster,

Returning home.

FINDING NEW PLACES...

A tall Nisei with powerful shoulders, who was leaning against the wall and talking to a baggage man, chucked his cigarette away and approached the group. "You folks travelin' too?" he said pleasantly. "Anyone goin' my way...Akron, Ohio?"

A dapper Nisei chuckled softly. "It seems we have different choices. This fellow here is going to study in Madison, Wisconsin, and, of course, this soldier is going to Shelby, Mississippi. And I'm heading for New York. By the way, where is that Issei woman with the child going?"

"She's going to Missouri...Kansas City," said the soldier.

"And where are you girls going'?" asked the Nisei with the hefty shoulders, turning to the two Nisei girls.

"I am going to Chicago...a job is waiting for me in the office of a big firm, and she," indicating her companion, "is getting married in Philadelphia."

The Nisei with the powerful shoulders shifted his weight from one foot to the other. "Chicago...Philadelphia...Kansas City...New York...Camp Shelby...Madison...Akron. Boy, we Nisei are certainly traveling nowadays. We're like seeds in the wind."

Toshio Mori, **"The Travellers"**

REBUILDING FROM NOTHING...

In October of 1945, Mother returned with the family to Los Osos to find their yard and home in total disarray. Weeds were so high, they could hardly see their home. The door was partly off the hinge and would not close. What had been locked upstairs in a room, had been stolen or thrown out of the window.

Mother found the remnants of the beautiful *O Hina Sama* dolls she used to display each year on Girl's Day broken and strewn on the ground.

Nothing could be planted in the fields because the tomato crop was being harvested by the tenants, and they did not want to give this up. Mother, Father and my brother and his family had to make a new beginning.

At age fifty-six, Mother was again helping on the farm as it slowly became reestablished, bunching broccoli, asparagus, or packing tomatoes.

"We have been through worse times," she said. "This is nothing."

Grace Shibata, **Okaasan**

IN A CHANGED COUNTRY...

The stories, the murmurs, the headlines of the last few months had imprinted in my mind the word HATE. I had heard my sisters say, "Why do they hate us?" I had heard Mama say with lonesome resignation, "I don't understand all this hate in the world."

It was a bleak and awful-sounding word, yet I had no idea at all what shape it might take if ever I confronted it. I saw it as a dark, amorphous cloud that would descend from above and enclose us forever. As we entered Los Angeles, I sat huddled in the back seat, silent, fearing any word I uttered might bring it to life.

But there was no sign of it anywhere, in fact no response to us at all as we drove down the palm-lined boulevards, past the busy rows of shops and markets, the lawns and driveways of quiet residential streets.

[When we left in 1942], no one had any idea what to expect, since no one knew what awaited us; we had been unprepared and that just deepened the shock of what we found.

[But] now the situation was reversed. In the isolated world of our camp we had overprepared for shows of abuse. If anything, what greeted us now was indifference.

Indeed, if the movements of this city were an indication, the existence of Manzanar and all it had stood for might be in doubt. The land we drove away from three and a half years earlier had not altered a bit.

Here we were, like fleeing refugees, trekking in from some ruined zone of war. And yet, on our six-hour drive south, we seemed to have passed through a time machine, as if, in March of 1942 one had lifted his foot to take a step, and set it down in October of 1945, and was expected just to keep on walking, with all intervening time erased.

Jeanne Wakatsuki Houston, **Farewell to Manzanar**

STRIPPED OF VALUE...

"During the *nikkei's* long internment, many homes and orchards did not fare well in the hands of local caretakers and renters. Some homes were vandalized; others were completely stripped of anything of value, from toilet fixtures to windows. Copper wire was ripped from the walls. The farms and orchards had suffered damage it would take years of hard work to repair. Asparagus fields were choked with two-foot high weeds. Apple trees, unpruned for four seasons, looked like weeping willows, with branches hanging so low that a person could sit on the ground and pick fruit."

Lauren Kessler, **Stubborn Twig**

CHAPTER

IX

War and change,
My native land
Once so hard to leave,
Is behind me now
forever.

Forgetting

A NEW WORLD OPENS...

"The first president of the United States was Jo-ji Wa-shin-ton. July 4, 1776 was the day that America declared independence from Britain; there are 50 states but originally there were 13. Do you know who discovered America? Columbus. In 1492."

Mama sat proudly in her usual manner with legs tucked under and hands folded gently on her lap. She was determined to get her citizenship.

"I never plan to return to Japan. My children and grandchildren are all American citizens. I do not belong in Japan. There is nothing for me there." Her facial muscles relaxed as her thoughts drifted back to her homeland. "I can't go back. Let's just keep that a dream."

That's what Japan symbolized to her now. A dream. And as I sat back into the couch and silently watched her review the lessons for her Sunday afternoon citizenship classes, it occurred to me that exactly 57 years ago America was the dream: a land of opportunity, an adventure to be experienced.

Akemi Kikumura, **Through Harsh Winters**

"Oh," Okaa-chan stops and thinks. She shakes her head impatiently, as if trying to shake a dormant memory into wakefulness. "Let's see, maybe two weeks? We could bring what we could carry. Everything else had to be sold or given away." Okaa-chan trails off and looks at us with worry. She is disappointed by her memory and afraid that we will be disappointed with her.

When Okaa-chan speaks of her years in Relocation Camp, her voice is often hesitant. Often it fades: confused and apologetic. Her recollections are strangely lifeless.

In this way, the Wyoming desert, with its cruel extremes, with its aching cold and killing heat, still holds my mother against her will.

Lydia Minatoya, **Talking to High Monks in the Snow**

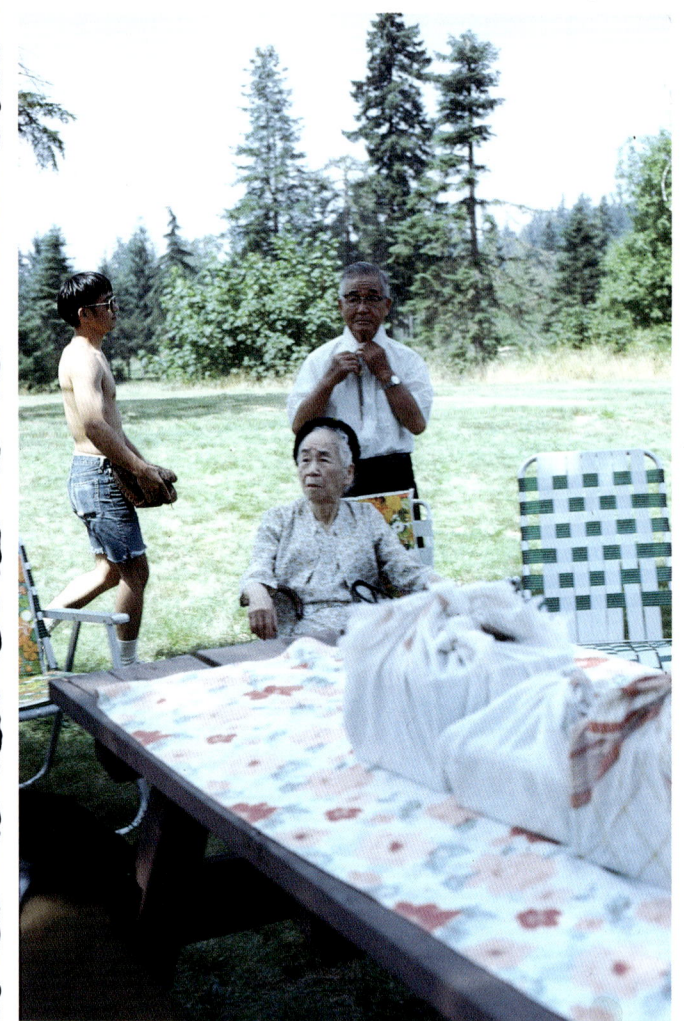

THE NEIGHBORHOOD GONE...

They moved out to the Avenues, leaving the dark corridors and background music of mixed tongues for a sturdy little house in a predominantly *hakujin* neighborhood, where everyone had a yard enclosed by a fence.

Sealed off in her little house in the fog-shrouded Avenues, the past seemed like a dream. Her parents, the old Victorian house, the shuffling of slippered guests, and the low mumble of Japanese, all gone from her life.

Her college friends were scattered all over the country, or married and sealed off in their own private worlds. But she felt no sense of loss. Their lives, after all, were getting better. There was no time to look back on those days before the war.

R.A. Sasaki, **The Loom**

CHAPTER
X

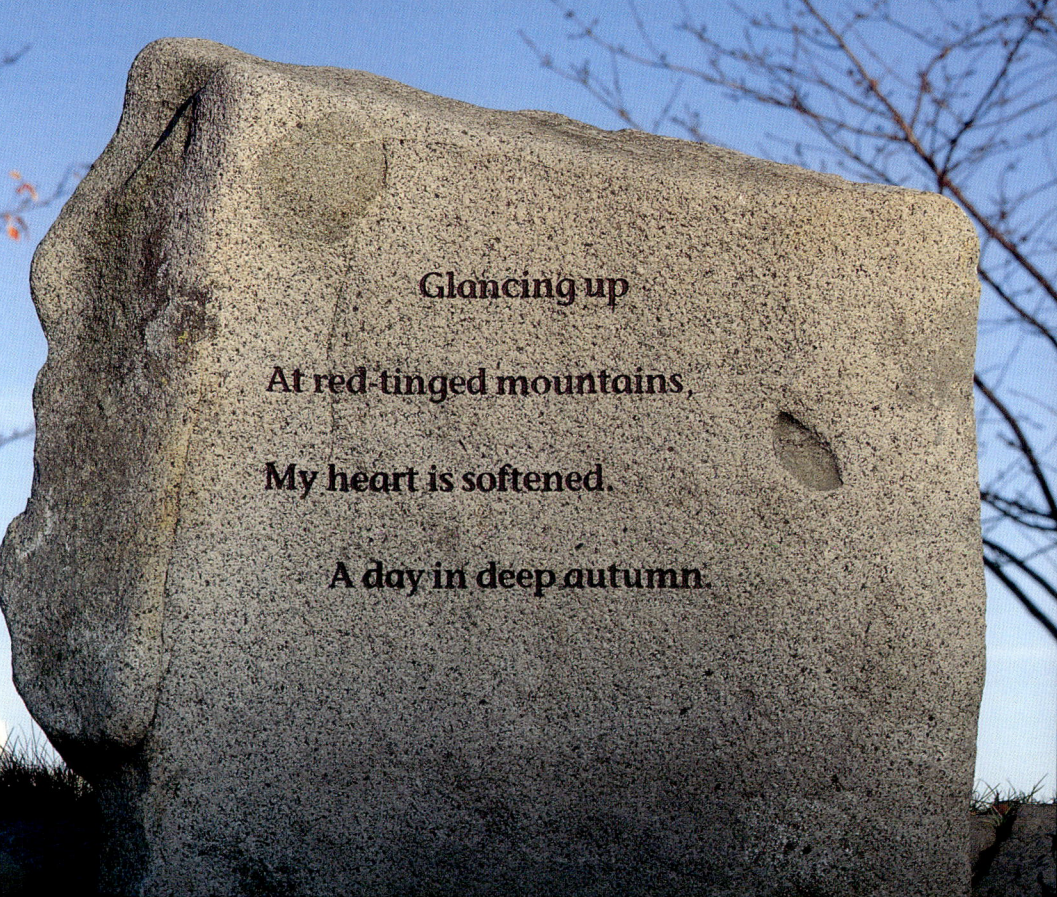

Healing

A MATTER OF ATTITUDE...

This is the way it ought to be, he thought to himself, to be able to dance with a girl you like and really get a kick out of it because everything is on an even keel and one's worries are only the usual ones of unpaid bills and sickness in the family and being late to work too often.

Why can't it be that way for me? Nobody's looking twice at us. Nobody's asking me where I was during the war or what the hell I am doing back on the Coast.

There's no trouble to be had without looking for it. Everything's the same, just as it used to be. No bad feelings except for those that have always existed and probably always will.

It's a matter of attitude.

Mine needs changing. I've got to love the world the way I used to. I've got to love it and the people so I'll feel good, and feeling good will make life worthwhile. There's no point crying about what's done...I want only to go on living and be happy. I've only to let myself do so.

John Okada, **No-No Boy**

FORGIVE WITHOUT FORGETTING...

"You've cause for anger, Mr. Oka," said Stephen Olssen. "But try now to forgive us if you can. Don't destroy yourself with any more bitterness."

The old man looked startled. "Forgive you?" he asked.

"Yes, all of us...if you can."

"Can you forgive the Japanese soldiers who killed your only son?"

"I have already."

Mr. Oka shook his head. "Forgive..." he murmured. The word came slowly and softly from his lips as though he were understanding it for the first time. He spoke the word as a blind man might feel a new object, touching it, discovering it, wondering about it, amazed at the feelings that came alive as he said the word.

Then he said slowly, "I guess forgiving does take the bundle of hate off your back. Still, when you've been wronged for so many years..." Mr. Oka paused. "Well, maybe there are ways to fight back without destroying yourself. I suppose we need to forgive ourselves, just as much as other people," he said.

Yoshiko Uchida, **Journey Home**

HOPES AND DREAMS...

As I sit out on the balcony by myself and look out over the ocean, images of my past arise as an enveloping mist to fill my mind. Someone said, "When one recalls experiences of the past, they light up in themselves to be like dreams." My dreams, quite definitely, span many changes and different backdrops. Filled with impossible hopes, encountering obstacles to attaining such hopes, then resurrecting such hopes again, the days of my past form a continuum. Now, looking back at earlier days, I feel no regrets. After all this, I feel, it is well that I have had this life.

Seiichi Higashide, **Adios to Tears**

ADMITTING MISTAKES...

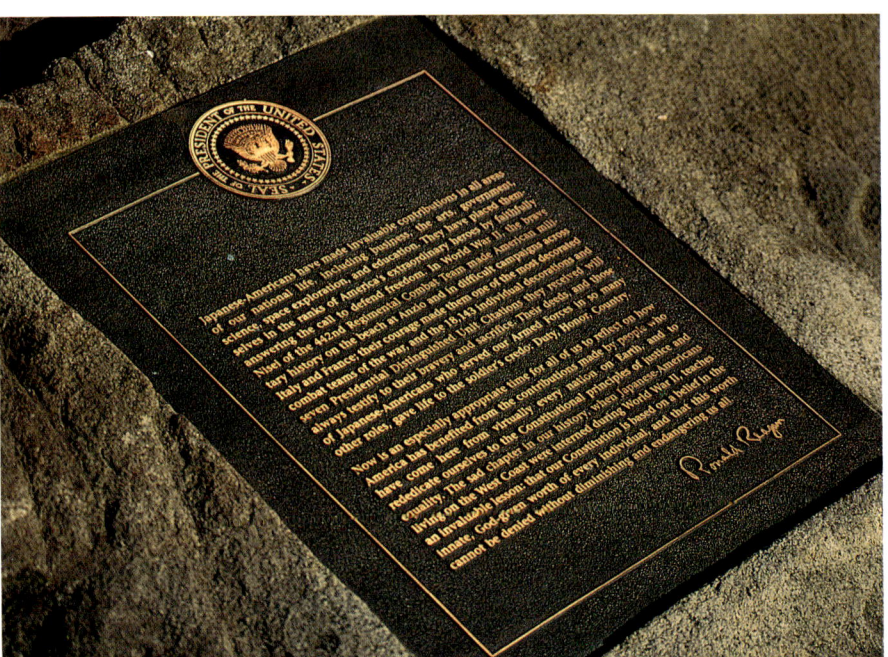

"On August 10, 1988, the long battle for redress officially ended when President Ronald Reagan signed into law the Civil Liberties Act of 1988. It called for the government to issue individual apologies for all violations of civil liberties and constitutional rights, backing up the words with $20,000 tax-free payments to each internment survivor.

"It's not for us to pass judgment upon those who may have made mistakes while engaged in World War II," Reagan told an audience of two hundred of the bill's most ardent supporters gathered to watch the signing. "Yet we must recognize that the internment of Japanese Americans was just that, a mistake." Later in his brief speech the president came on stronger: "What is important in this bill has less to do with property than with honor, for here we admit a wrong. Here, we reaffirm our commitment as a nation to equal justice under the law."

Lauren Kessler, **Stubborn Twig**

CHAPTER
XI

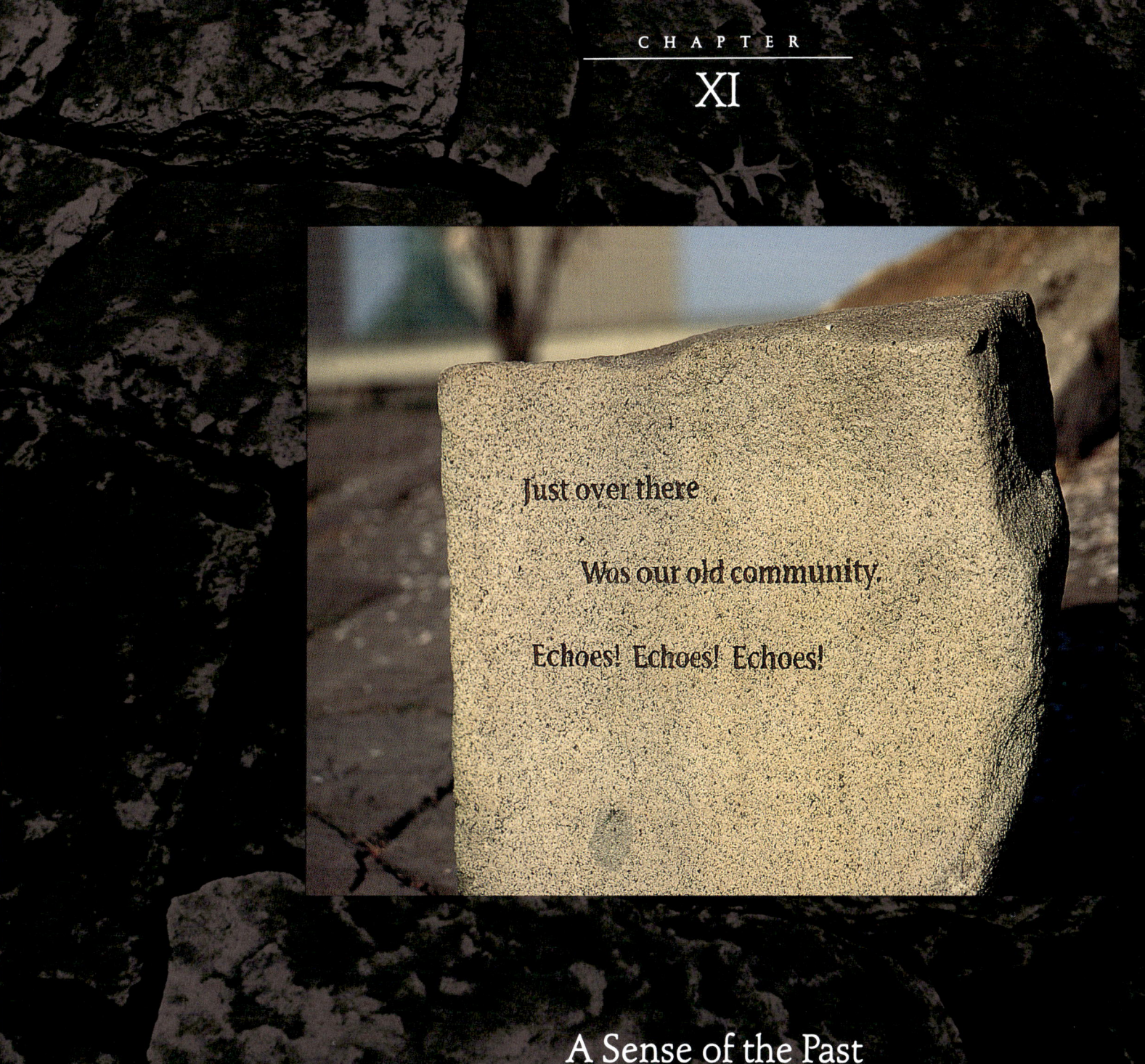

A Sense of the Past

FAMILY HISTORY...

I brought our family genealogy back when I made a trip to Japan. I showed it to my children and grandchildren. They were deeply impressed by it.

I showed them when our family line started, and they were amazed.

At one time I advocated the following: What about making a genealogy of the Issei, Nisei, and Sansei? We Japanese didn't appear in the United States by accident. It would be interesting for the future.

The Nisei, who observed their fathers as youngsters, still don't realize how hard their fathers struggled. They are too subjective to realize what the Issei actually have done.

The Sansei are amazed at how great their grandfathers were. The Sansei question themselves about whether they could do the same things that their grandfathers had in the past, and they come to the realization that what their grandfathers had done wasn't easy.

Yoshito Fujii, **oral history**

almost as if the graves they care for are more than graves of the infants and elderly, who while living in this desolate enclave so terrified the rest of America.

It is as though they were the graves of the pilgrims' civil and constitutional rights.

William Minoru Hohri, **America Repaired**

CONTINUITY...

They spoke of a reunion, a reunion of the Del Rey Japanese American community, a gathering of the past and present residents and a renewal of friendships. Their paramount concern: they had to meet before the old ones died. The "old ones" used to mean the Issei but now the Nisei had entered those ranks and a sense of mortality found a way into their thinking.

At first it was to be a gathering of the old community, with only the Issei and Nisei.

"Why would the Sansei want to come to a reunion?" they asked.

Yet perhaps more than anyone else, the Sansei needed that sense of history, a sense of home and community.

After some discussion the Sansei were allowed to come and the reunion was transformed into something different. It became a reunion of family, of children returning home for a journey into the past.

David Masumoto, **Country Voices**

CHAPTER

XII

With new hope,

We build new lives.

Why complain when it rains?

This is what it means to be free.

Looking Ahead

THE LAST STONE...

This last chapter, the thirteenth stone, stands for the voices not yet heard, the words not yet spoken, the generations not yet arrived.

It is a stone of hope, for a legacy of acceptance and not of isolation, of remembering and not of forgetting, of accomplishment and not of loss.

The lives of future generations will come, their voices will be heard. Let them answer the voices of their ancestors as they retell the stories of their families, their people, their country.

Let them, too, touch their hands to the stones. Let them, too, know what it means to be free.

EPILOGUE

The idea of creating a tribute to the Japanese American pioneers began to form in my mind about the time we returned to the United States in 1976 after spending ten years in Japan. After pursuing the idea with the Japanese American Citizens League in the early eighties, I met Bill Naito, a Portland civic leader and city visionary, who not only was supportive of the idea but, more importantly, had the political clout to make it happen. As we discussed possible sites for this concept, we learned that the City of Portland was planning improvements for the northern portion of Tom McCall Waterfront Park. This particular site happened to be across the street from what was once the pre-war Japantown and was located between two of Portland's major river crossings, the historic Steel Bridge and the Burnside Bridge. Given these conditions, it was an ideal site for the memorial. A non-profit group, the Oregon Nikkei Endowment, headed by Henry Sakamoto, was formed to sponsor the project.

I felt that the basis for the design of this tribute should come not only from Japan's aesthetic traditions but should embrace the American landscape heritage as well. I felt that the memorial should not be a place that could be described as pretty, attractive, clever, a traditional park or a lyrical picture—but, instead that it be a slice of life which interprets the Japanese American experience with emotion and cultural sensitivity and without sentiment.

The inspiration of other special places and images came to mind as I started the design process. With a few simple but extraordinary design moves, Maya Lin brought about the most profound and moving landscape experience of this century with the Vietnam Memorial. The stone sculpture and gardens of Isamu Noguchi have always stimulated and influenced my way of seeing just as Akira Kurosawa's sweeping images in his films have haunted my memories. Kurosawa's compositions in black and white have a richness, a sense of starkness and mystery like a wonderful Japanese Muromachi-period garden. His classic film, the Seven Samurai, has a moving scene in which the samurai are paying homage to one of their fallen warriors. An earthen burial mound with a sword piercing the earth, positioned against the vast sky, is a powerful image which influenced the "touch" of the memorial's central stones.

Having studied in Kyoto, Japan's ancient capital whose city plan was derived from Ch'angan, the old capital of China, I understood the impor-

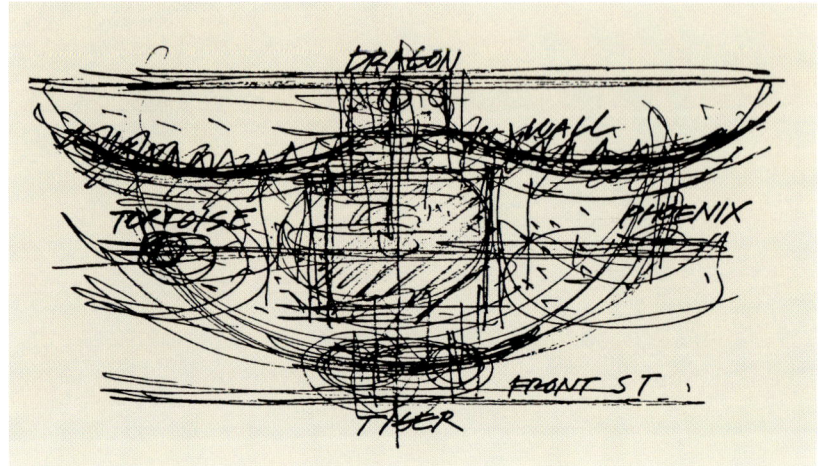

tance of this geomantic tradition of site planning to maintain harmony between man and nature. The memorial reflects this relationship. To the *east,* the *dragon* gateway and wall are formed of rough-hewn basalt stones which curve along the Willamette River. The *western* gateway, the *tiger,* is marked with two bronze columns sculptured by Jim Gion. They visually describe the history of Japanese Americans from the early Issei immigration to the present. To the *north* is the *tortoise,* where a large stone is set on a low earthen mound. This recalls the legend of mystic islands where the immortals were supported on the backs of giant turtles. The *south* entry is perceived as the legendary *phoenix* and this is where the Japanese story begins.

Singular large granite stones symbolize the Japanese immigrants coming to Oregon, and, like the evolving Japanese American community, the stones gradually become a wall, solid and whole. Rising from the wall, twelve standing granite stones and their inscriptions speak to us in poetry.

The voices continue to the break in the wall, where the story of the Japanese American community is disrupted by mass evacuation and relocation during the war. Three stones break away from the wall and rise out of the fractured paving, reflecting broken lives and shattered dreams. The large standing stone in the center of the plaza has the inscribed names of the ten relocation camps. The center of the plaza also represents mother earth, a place which has the power and ambiance to restore and nourish the soul. The wall continues and reflects the years following the war, a period which has been a time of healing and rebuilding.

The essence of the Plaza was captured by a poem written by K.O. Lee shortly after the opening:

> *The Plaza visits and revisits me*
>
> > *All at the same moment*
> > *proud/sad and happy was I*
>
> > *K.O. Lee: U.S. citizen*
> > *affirmed and reaffirmed am I*
>
> > *Burning and churning gone*
> > *learning and relearning on.*
>
> *The Plaza visits and revisits me*
>
> > *Being honored and blessed*
> > *even forgiven and forgiving was I*
>
> > *K.O. Lee: world citizen*
> > *charged and recharged am I*
>
> > *More than grateful and thankful*
> > *my heart and soul…peaceful*
>
> *The Plaza visits and revisits me.*

Robert Murase, *Landscape Architect*

ABOUT THE AUTHORS

Seiichi Higashide
Born in 1904 on the island of Hokkaido, Japan. In 1930 he established roots in Peru. Within ten years he started a family and became a successful businessman. World War II brought about many adversities, resulting in his arrest, deportation and detention in the United States. Following his release, he overcame additional hardships and eventually came to love and adopt his third "motherland."

William Minoru Hohri
A Nisei of Westwood, California before the war. Hohri was interned at Manzanar, California. He resettled in Chicago, Illinois. In 1988, while serving as chairperson of the National Council for Japanese American Redress, he published **Repairing America: An Account of the Movement for Japanese-American Redress.**

Bill Hosokawa
Born and raised in Seattle, he became a journalist with English-language newspapers in Singapore and Shanghai before the war. After returning to Seattle, Hosokawa was interned at Heart Mountain, Wyoming. He resettled in Des Moines, Iowa, then Denver. He continues to write "The Frying Pan" column for the Pacific Citizen, and is the author of several books. He is quoted in this text from the 1978 anthology **Thirty-Five Years in the Frying Pan.**

Jeanne Wakatsuki Houston
A Nisei born in Inglewood, California. She was interned at Manzanar, California. Later she attended college in San Jose, California. After marrying James Houston in 1957, she travelled widely during his U.S. Air Force duty, eventually settling in Santa Cruz, California. **Farewell to Manzanar** was co-authored by the couple in 1973.

Akemi Kikumura
A Nisei, born in California after her family had returned from internment at Rohwer, Arkansas. In 1981, having received a Ph.D. in anthropology from UCLA, she published the memoirs of her Issei mother, Michiko Tanaka in **Through Harsh Winters: The Life of a Japanese Immigrant Woman.** Her father's story is the subject of her more recent book, **Promises Kept.**

Lauren Kessler
Born in New York and received her bachelor's degree from Northwestern University in Evanston, Illinois, and her Ph.D. from the University of Washington. Her graduate work was in American History. She is the author of seven books, including **After All These Years,** a social history of the 1960s, and **The Dissident Press,** a history of minority journalism. Her award-winning writings on the Japanese American experience have appeared in both magazines and scholarly journals. She teaches at the University of Oregon.

Mitzi Asai Loftus
A Nisei born in Hood River, Oregon. She was interned at Tule Lake, California and later Heart Mountain, Wyoming. She returned to Hood River, Oregon after the war. Later, she spent a year in Japan and two years in Germany before returning to Oregon to raise her family. She published her memoirs, **Made In Japan and Settled in Oregon,** while living in Coos Bay, Oregon in 1990.

Mike Masaoka
Born in California, and educated in Salt Lake City. He achieved national recognition for his debating skills before the war, and rose to a position of leadership in the Japanese American Citizens League. A spokesman for his generation, he served with the 442nd Regimental Combat Team during the war. He represented the JACL in Washington, D.C. for the next thirty years. His memoirs, written with Bill Hosokawa, were published in 1987 as **They Call Me Moses Masaoka: An American Saga.**

David Mas Masumoto
A Sansei, he grew up in the farming community of Del Rey, California after his family was released from Gila River, Arizona. He has published numerous articles and stories, for which he won the James Clavell National Japanese American Literary Award in 1986. In 1987, still writing and farming in Del Rey, he published **Country Voices: The Oral History of a Japanese American Family Farm Community.**

Lydia Yuriko Minatoya
A Sansei, born in 1950, raised in the Eastern U.S., where her family resettled after internment at Heart Mountain, Wyoming. Following her formal education, Minatoya spent several years travelling throughout Asia. Her 1992 memoirs of her family, childhood and travels are published as **Talking to High Monks in the Snow.** She lives in Seattle, Washington with her husband and two children.

Edward Miyakawa
A Nisei, born in Sacramento, California in 1934. Miyakawa was interned at Tule Lake, California for one year, then resettled in Boulder, Colorado. His 1979 novel, **Tule Lake** is based on the experiences of others who remained at Tule Lake as "disloyals."

Toshio Mori
Born in Oakland, California in 1910, Toshio Mori is the first Japanese American short story writer to be published in the U.S. Mori was interned at Topaz, Utah. He resettled in San Leandro, California after the war. He has written hundreds of short stories, and several novels. Selections in this volume are taken from the 1949 short story collection **Yokohama, California;** and **The Chauvinist and Other Stories** published in 1979.

Kaoru C. Nomura
Born in Deer Lodge, Montana and grew up in Los Angeles. Earned a Ph.D. in physics at the University of Minnesota and an AMP from the Harvard Graduate School of Business Administration. Starting as a researcher in the physics of the solid state, he rose to Corporate Senior Vice President of Honeywell, Inc. He is the recipient of many awards. Among them is the University of Minnesota's highest award, the Distinguished Graduate/Outstanding Achievement Award. In his retirement, the community of Port Townsend, Washington is building the "K.C. Nomura Building" for his unselfish dedication to and successful establishment of businesses that hire the mentally handicapped, school dropouts, and brain damaged youth in the community.

ORAL HISTORY QUOTATIONS

Gene Oishi
A Nisei raised in Guadalupe, California, Oishi was a young child when he was interned at Gila, Arizona. He resumed his education in Guadalupe after the war, pursued a career in journalism, eventually serving in the Washington press corps during the Nixon administration. He reached a certain notoriety when Vice-President Spiro Agnew referred to him as a "Jap," within the hearing of other reporters. In 1988 Oishi published his memoirs, **In Search of Hiroshi: A Japanese-American Odyssey.**

John Okada
A Nisei, born in Seattle, Washington in 1923. He attended University of Washington and Columbia University in New York before serving in the U.S. Army during World War II. He returned to Seattle, where he died in 1947 after writing **No No Boy.** The book was rejected during his lifetime, and first published in 1957 by a small press. Hardly noticed, it was eventually rediscovered and republished in 1977, and now recognized as a major Asian-American novel.

Mine Okubo
A Nisei, born in 1912 in Riverside, California. She studied art at University of California, Berkeley, receiving an M.A. Okubo was interned at Topaz, Utah. She resettled in New York where, in 1946, her line drawings and memoirs were published as **Citizen 13660.** In more recent years she has concentrated on her work in fine arts, and has exhibited frequently in one-woman and group shows.

R.A. Sasaki
A third-generation San Franciscan. Sasaki's family was interned at Topaz, Utah. She has an M.A. in Creative Writing from San Francisco State University, and has published numerous short stories, winning the American Japanese National Literary Award in 1983. Her first published collection is **The Loom and Other Stories** (Graywolf Press, 1991).

Grace Shibata
A Nisei, born Grace Eto in 1925, the youngest of eight children raised in the farming community of Los Osos, California. She was interned with her family at Manzanar, California. The family resettled at Los Osos after the war. Shibata's biography of her mother, **Okaasan,** was published in 1990 as a chapter of **Japanese American Women: Three Generations 1890-1990,** by Mei Nakano.

Monica Sone
A Nisei, born and raised in Seattle, Washington, one of four children. Sone was interned at Minidoka, Idaho. She resettled as a student at Wendell College in southern Indiana. In 1953 she published her memoirs as **Nisei Daughter.** It is still among the most widely read books by any Japanese American writer.

Dorothy Swaine Thomas
She is a sociologist at the University of California, Berkeley. With the help of other professors and graduate students, she conducted a large, multidisciplinary research project on Japanese Americans who were interned during World War II. **The Salvage** was one aspect of the study. It was published in 1952 and focused on those who left camps and resettled in the Midwest and East.

Yoshiko Uchida
A Nisei, raised in Berkeley, California. She was in college at the University of California, Berkeley when her family was evacuated. Uchida was interned at Topaz, Utah. She left camp to enroll at Smith College in Massachusetts, where she completed a master's degree. As a children's author, Uchida has published more than a dozen titles, including **Journey Home,** in 1978, about her internment experience. In 1982, she published her memoirs for adult readers, **Desert Exile: The Uprooting of a Japanese-American Family.**

Yoshito Fujii
Born in Hiroshima-ken, Japan in 1900. Emigrated at age 19. Settled in Seattle, Washington, pursued a college education before entering business. Arrested after Pearl Harbor and held in North Dakota, then transferred to Puyallup Assembly Center in Washington. Interned at Minidoka, Idaho, then returned to Seattle. Interviewed in 1973 by **Issei Oral History Project.**

Gordon Hirabayashi
He grew up in Washington State, and was a 24 year old student at the University of Washington at the outbreak of World War II. Hirabayashi chose to protest the curfew order in order to challenge its legality. The courts ruled against him, and he remained imprisoned throughout the war. In 1943 his case was heard at the Supreme Court, and his conviction upheld. Not until 1987 was his conviction overturned by the federal courts in Seattle. Hirabayashi was interviewed for the 1992 documentary film, **"A Personal Matter: Hirabayashi v. The United States."** Hirabayashi, a retired sociology professor, lives in Edmonton, Canada.

Masao Hirata
Born in Kumamoto-ken, Japan in 1903. In 1920 he joined his father as a farm laborer in California. He was married and had six children when he was arrested and taken to New Mexico. His family was interned at Poston, Arizona. He resettled in California after the war. He was interviewed at age 71 by the **Issei Oral History Project.**

Wataru Ishisaka
Born 1906 in Kumamoto-ken, Japan. He emigrated in 1923 and married a Nisei in California, where he settled as a farmer. He was interned at Granada, Colorado. Resettling in Sacramento, California after the war, he died in spring of 1978. He was interviewed by the **Issei Oral History Project.**

Frank Kadowaki
He was born in Shimane, Japan in the late 1880s. His parents had both emigrated by the time he was eight. He joined them ten years later in Santa Ana, California. He was a farmer, but trained as an artist. He was interned at Poston, Arizona, then relocated to New York where he began pursuing a career in the fine arts. His interview and

FURTHER NOTES

paintings are presented in **Beyond Words: Images from America's Concentration Camps.**

Yoshisada Kawai
Born 1889 in Hiroshima-ken, Japan. He was 17 years old when he immigrated to the Northwestern U.S. He worked as a mechanic and machine operator. Mr. Kawai was interned at Minidoka, Idaho, eventually resettling in Seattle, Washington. He was 81 years old when he interviewed in writing with the **Issei Oral History Project** in 1970.

Jack Matsuoka
Born 1925, raised in Watsonville, California. He was interned in Poston, Arizona at age seventeen. He resettled in Cleveland, Ohio, where he began pursuing a career in the arts. After being drafted into the Army and stationed in Japan, Matsuoka returned to California, married, and became successful as a political cartoonist. His early cartoons from Poston have been published as **Camp II, Block 21.** His interview appears in **Beyond Words.**

Lawrence Sasano
Raised in Los Angeles, California, he was pursuing a career in photography when he was interned at Poston, Arizona. Sasano left camp to join the Army, serving in the Pacific. He returned to Los Angeles. His interview, along with drawings he produced at Poston, are published in **Beyond Words.**

Mary Tsukamoto
Born in California, her family operated a laundry in San Francisco, later moving out of the city to farm strawberries. She was married and was with her five year old daughter when interned at Jerome, Arkansas. In 1984 her oral history was recorded in **And Justice For All,** by John Tateishi.

Takae Washizu
Born 1900 in Aichi Prefecture, Japan. She married at 21 and came with her husband to the U.S. the same year. She workd with him as a farm laborer and raised three children. Interned in Granada, Colorado. The family then divided to find employment, rejoining eventually. Mrs. Washizu was interviewed by the **Issei Oral History Project.**

About the Poetry
The twelve poems heading each chapter are taken from the Japanese American Historical Plaza in Portland, Oregon. The poets are not identified at the memorial itself, in order to emphasize the collective voices that tell the history of the Japanese American people.

Lawson Inada of Ashland, Oregon, **Hisako Saito** and **Masaki Kinoshita** of Portland, Oregon, and the family of the late **Shizue Iwatsuki** of Hood River, Oregon agreed to the anonymity of their work at the memorial. A poem by **K.O. Lee** also appears in the Epilogue.

About Authors Not Included
This book does not claim to represent the entire range of Japanese American writings. Of particular note: Hisaye Yamamoto, whose stories proved difficult to excerpt; Joy Kogawa, who is Japanese Canadian and sadly excluded from this volume for sake of consistency; many Japanese American writers from Hawaii who have written of the unusual experiences of Japanese Hawaiians during the Second World War. There are also several Japanese American playwrights of note, whose works are unfortunately too difficult to include among the prose samples of this text.

In short, **Touching The Stones** can only claim to scratch the surface of available writings on the Japanese American story. Our sincere hope is that many readers of this book will be encouraged to browse through their local library shelves to discover the legacy of Japanese American writers, historians, poets, dramatists, and story-tellers.

INDEX OF SOURCES

CHAPTER ONE
Lawson Inada, poem

Yoshisada Kawai, from *Issei Christians: Selected Interviews from the Issei Oral History Project,* Eileen Sunada Sarasohn editor, (Issei Oral History Project, Inc., 1977), p. 6

Toshio Mori, "Tomorrow is Long, Children," *Yokohama, California* (Caxton Printers, 1949), p. 17

Akemi Kikumura, *Through Harsh Winters: The Life of an Immigrant Japanese-American Woman* (Chandler & Sharp Publishers, 1981), p. 31-32

Lydia Yuriko Minatoya, *Talking to High Monks in the Snow: An Asian American Odyssey* HarperCollins Publishers, Inc. 1992), p. 18-19

CHAPTER TWO
Lawson Inada, poem

John Okada, *No-No Boy* (third edition, University of Washington Press, 1976), p. 15-16

Monica Sone, *Nisei Daughter* (Little Brown and Company, 1953), p. 3-4

Bill Hosokawa, "The Frying Pan" September 1946, reprinted in **Thirty-Five Years in the Frying Pan** (McGraw-Hill Book Company, 1978), p. 84

Dorothy Swaine Thomas, *The Salvage,* (University of California Press, 1952) p. 326

Kaoru C. Nomura, *Family Stories* (Published for a family reunion in 1994), p. 64

CHAPTER THREE
Lawson Inada, poem

Mine Okubo, *Citizen 13660* (Columbia University Press, 1946), p. 10-12

Jack Matsuoka, interviewed for *Beyond Words: Images from America's Concentration Camps,* Deborah Gesenway and Mindy Roseman editors (Cornell Univesity Press, 1987), p. 136

William Minoru Hohri, *Repairing America: An Account of the Movement for Japanese-American Redress* (Washington State University Press, 1988), p. 16-17

Hisako Saito, poem

Masao Hirata, interview for *The Issei: Portrait of a Pioneer, An Oral History,* Eileen Sunada Sarasohn editor (Pacific Books, Publishers, 1983 by the Issei Oral History Project), p. 162

CHAPTER FOUR

Shizue Iwatsuki, poem

Jeanne Wakatsuki Houston, *Farewell to Manzanar,* with James Houston (Houghton Mifflin Company, 1973), p. 12-13

Takae Washizu, interview for *The Issei: Portrait of a Pioneer,* p. 166

Yoshiko Uchida, *Desert Exile: The Uprooting of a Japanese-American Family* (University of Washington Press, 1982), p. 70-71

R.A. Sasaki, *The Loom and Other Stories* (Graywolf Press, 1991), p. 24

CHAPTER FIVE

Shizue Iwatsuki, poem

Edward Miyakawa, *Tule Lake* (House By The Sea Publishing Company, 1979), p. 88

Monica Sone, *Nisei Daughter,* p. 192-193

Lawrence Sasano, interview for *Beyond Words,* p. 53

Gordon Hirabayashi, interview for **A Personal Matter: Hirabayashi v. The United States,** a documentary film transcript (The Constitution Project, 1989 by William Mandis), p. 11

CHAPTER SIX

Lawson Inada, poem

John Okada, *No-No Boy,* p. 34

Mike Masaoka, *They Call Me Moses Masaoka: An American Saga,* with Bill Hosokawa (William Morrow and Company, Inc., 1987), p. 23

Lydia Y. Minatoya, *Talking to High Monks in the Snow,* p. 43

William M. Hohri, *Repairing America,* p. 2

TEN CAMPS

Gene Oishi, *In Search of Hiroshi: A Japanese-American Odyssey* (Charles E. Tuttle Company, Inc., 1988), p. 54-55

Wataru Ishisaka, interview for *The Issei,* p. 204

Bill Hosokawa, "The Frying Pan" November 1944, or *Thirty-Five Years in the Frying Pan,* p. 32

Mary Tsukamoto, interview for *And Justice For All,* John Tateishi editor (Random House, Inc., 1984), p. 14

Jeanne W. Houston, *Farewell to Manzanar,* pg. 85

Monica Sone, *Nisei Daughter,* p. 196-197

Frank Kadowaki, interview for *Beyond Words,* p. 88

Akemi Kikumura, *Through Harsh Winters,* p. 52

Yoshiko Uchida, *Desert Exile,* p. 137-138

Edward Miyakawa, *Tule Lake,* p. 187-188

CHAPTER SEVEN

Shizue Iwatsuki, poem

Gene Oishi, *In Search of Hiroshi,* p. 75-76

Mitzi Asai Loftus, *Made In Japan and Settled in Oregon* (Pigeon Point Press, 1990), p. 129-130

Mine Okubo, *Citizen 13660,* p. 208

CHAPTER EIGHT

Shizue Iwatsuki, poem

Toshio Mori, "The Travellers," *The Chauvinist and Other Stories* (U.C.L.A. Asian American Studies Center, 1979), p. 130-131

Grace Shibata, "Okaasan," published in *Japanese American Women: Three Generations 1890-1990,* Mei Nakano editor (Mina Press Publishers, 1990), p. 92

Jeanne W. Houston, *Farewell to Manzanar,* p. 131-132

Lauren Kessler, *The Stubborn Twig,* (Random House Publishing, 1993), p. 241

CHAPTER NINE

Shizue Iwatsuki, poem

Akemi Kikumura, *Through Harsh Winters,* p. 85

Lydia Y. Minatoya, *Talking to High Monks in the Snow,* p. 14

R.A. Sasaki, *The Loom and Other Stories,* p. 27

Masaki Kinoshita

CHAPTER TEN

Shizue Iwatsuki, poem

John Okada, *No-No Boy,* p. 209

Yoshiko Uchida, *Journey Home* (Atheneum, 1978), p. 125

Seiichi Higashide, *Adios to Tears* (E&E Kudo, 1993), p. 244

Lauren Kessler, *The Stubborn Twig,* p. 276

CHAPTER ELEVEN

Lawson Inada, poem

Yoshito Fujii, interview for *The Issei,* p. 270

William M. Hohri, *Repairing America,* p. 225-226

David Mas Masumoto, *Country Voices: The Oral History of a Japanese American Family Farm Community* (Inaka Countryside Publications, 1987), p. 78

CHAPTER TWELVE

Lawson Inada, poem

Textual Note:
Original texts may have been slightly altered in order to be presented in this volume. Some passages have been abbreviated. Some pronouns may have been clarified. In no case has a passage been rewritten to alter its meaning or literary effect.

EPILOGUE

K.O. Lee, poem

Acknowledgements

Bill Naito, for leadership and for generous allowances of his and his assistant's time while the manuscript has been in the making.

Robert and Judy Murase for time, energy, and vision during the development of this book.

Homer and Micki Yasui, for opening their home library for the research that made this book possible and for contributing historical photos.

The entire **Oregon Nikkei Endowment** board of directors for patience and confidence in this project.

Meyer Memorial Trust for a grant of $25,000.

To the hundreds of donors whose names are listed on the inside covers of the hardbound edition of this publication.

Photographic Credits

Photographers with page references of photographs:
Stephen Cridland: Cover, 82, 91
C. Bruce Forster: 10, 18, 26, 27, 28, 29, 37, 42, 43, 50, 52, 53, 58, 65, 66, 72, 73, 96, 97, 103
Joseph Erceg: 19, 34, 81, 88
Timothy Hursley: 6, 13, 21, 45, 74
Greg Kozawa: 11, 16, 17, 24, 25, 32, 33, 35, 40, 41, 48, 49, 51, 56, 57, 59, 70, 71, 78, 79, 86, 87, 89, 94, 95
Robert Murase: 80, 98, 102

Archival Collections with page and negative numbers:
Donald E. Estes and **Japanese American Citizens League:** 69, 100, 101, 105
National Japanese American Historical Society: 14, 30, 38, 55
Oregon Historical Society: 22 (#48760), 23 (#84821), 31-upper (#28157), 39 (#44601)
Seiichi Konno: 46
University of Washington Libraries: 15 (#523 and #15305), 31 (#1673), 54 (#15307)
Yasui Collection: 47, 68, 76, 77, 84, 85, 92, 93

We thank all of the individuals throughout the area who took time to pose for photographs. We regret that we were not able to include all of the subjects in this publication. We also express our appreciation to those who contributed photographs from their personal albums.

Memorial Design Team

Designer: Robert K. Murase, FASLA
Project Team: Alan Johnson, Greg Covey
Poetry: Lawson Inada
Sculptor: Jim Gion
Graphics: Elizabeth Anderson, Isamu Iwamoto
Research: Mark Sherman
Stonemasons: Masatoshi Izumi, Ed Locket, Bill Brashear

The stones in this book can be found in the Japanese American Historical Plaza which is located in Portland, Oregon at the north end of Tom McCall Waterfront Park, Northwest Couch Street and Front Avenue.